number one adventure of a
small black bear

number one adventure of a
small black bear

transcribed from a pocket book
belonging to Ossip Ossip and lost in the
woods

My apologies to:

Celine Dion

Professor Rubic

The Hungarian Institute of Sciences

The New Venue and the people of Thurrock

The Dartford Crossing Authority

Portaloo

Mrs Gravell

Anyone called Demeter

Anyone (just write your name down)

hiya

What was Ossip doing on the top of the tarpaulin of a 40 ft articulated trailer laden with another consignment of defective Rubic cubes and travelling at speed down the M25 motorway towards the Thames at Dartford?

'A clear night' said Ossip 'is the ideal time to view Ursa Minor.'

'Being minor myself.'

So saying he stuck out his black-haired chest one paw on his junior astronomers telescope the other to salute the passer-by.

Poor Ossip, he had not reckoned with his driver, Mr Gravell and the Hungarian Truck Racing Double Declutch Gearbox, Bouncer, as it was known in the garages of Pest.

Buda too, which in one sharp and totally expected jerk not only raised the speed of the truck to hurtle it across the bridge but also tossed Ossip off the truck, off the bridge and into a soft, ugh, squiggly box of left over 'amburgers that marked the outer boundary of Thurrock

Ugh.

It was either the 'amburgers or a very sore bottom.

It was also a big surprise for the small Hungarian astronomer.

'Goodbye telescope.'

'Goodbye truck?'

Would Mr Gravell miss him?

Would he humpf.

Not till he was declared missing possibly lost in action by an increasingly irate boss who with a thump of his desk fit to burst his braces declared.

'He must be found and brought back to the shores of the Danube.'

'Only Ossip can disentangle the Rubic cubes.'

The other driver's Rubbleov, Edbleavit, Goulasov to mention 3 could only look accusingly at Gravell who retired to the nearest thermal baths and instructed the fattest masseuse to

'Beat me, pummel me for I have lost Ossip'

The utter shame of it.

To have lost the Austro-Hungarian Empire was one thing. But Ossip.

Oh dear.

Meanwhile in darkest Thurrock.

Twilight dusk gave way to inky night.

Ossip staggered out of the 'amburger box onto racks of

industrial pipe, looped over railway lines, threaded through tunnels, under and over, under and over, with hardly a blade of nourishing grass to be seen.

He reached edge of the Thames.

Oh sad river edged with grey foam, streaks of oil, soggy cardboard boxes, and empty plastic bottles.

No way could Ossip wash off the 'amburger to replace it with a layer of grey oily river Thames plus cardboard.

He would sooner jump off the end of one of the many jetties and take his chance in the swirling current.

Which he promptly and foolishly did

On an ebb tide!

'A what?' said Ossip waking up to the sight of a rapidly disappearing Thurrock

Help (segítség) that's Hungarian.

But all the big ships and the smaller ones just loomed up at him as he passed rapidly by clinging to the most buoyant of the 'amburger buns and then loomed silently away.

Coming up for air and furiously calculating whether and when at this speed he would hit the mouth of the Danube and float down to his blessed Pest and Buda,

Ossip spotted a big rusty arrow screwed to the top of a buoy with the single word Canvey.

What is this Canvey?(authors note:Canvey means Canvey in Hungarian)

'Turn left.' said another arrow.

'Why not.'

Ossip turned the bun and surfed onto a stony gravel beach landing at the foot of a foot.

Clad in a shocking pink stiletto-heeled shoe.

Poor Demeter. Once, she vaguely remembered, 'I had

an invitation to meet Mr Rubic' who is notoriously fussy about the braininess of his visitors.

Since she had tried to present a paper to the Academy of Sciences on the Celina Dion class of stars, her descent to the small G plan caravanette huddled against the dyke wall, that stood between the Isle of Canvey and the sea, had been rapid and ignominious.

'Ah Polaris' cried a small voice from her toe.

With an acuteness she had been previously known for Demeter observed 'my toe is talking to me.'

'I am no toe' said the toe which had now turned into a small black bear.

I am a subscribing associate of the Hungarian Academy of Sciences I will have you know.

'If that is Polaris' he said, pointing at the stars, 'Then I have a long way to go.'

Demeter's thoughts were rattling on.

Now.

She remembered why she was wandering around the beach in the night.

Why she had forgotten to shut the caravanette door, which clacked back and forth in the wind.

She had a problem,

of great importance.

So important that the little furry black object calling itself a bear could be the gift of the goddess.

The perfect corsage.

'I will thank you not to call me a corsage.' cried a much ruffled Ossip as Demeter seized him and stuffed him into her cleavage.

'A courtier, a luminary, but never a corsage.'

'Oh shush' said Demeter, a new light in her eyes.

Now she could face all those other karaoke girls, at the Venue Thurrock under the bridge, with her Celina Dion impersonations.

So what if they called her the witch of Canvey.

Now she could cast her spell.

The corsage said.

'The Celina Dion class of stars? Never heard of them.'

And promptly went to sleep.

'No No No Ossip you cannot leave me till I have performed.'

Cried Demeter through a curtain of tears as she watched Ossip determinably stuff her second best and largest travelling handbag with the contents of the bun cupboard.

'Listen Ossip do this for me and I will get you back to Hungary even if I have to sell this ring' Demeter said, desperately waving her ruby ring.

'Pshaw glass Demeter.

Besides you told me yourself there are Hungarian lorry drivers combing Thurrock and asking every day at the tolls for me. I am needed in Pest.'

'But why oh why do they want a small black bear?'

Ignorant girl thought Ossip.

'Because only I can unravel the defective rubic cubes.

Only I Ossip have experienced Care in the Community. Only I have that skill.

Come with me. Come to Pest. You can be my housekeeper Demeter. This caravan is no place for a girl like you.'

'Its no use Ossip. I want to sing. I need to fulfil myself and I need you. My pink dress needs you.'

'I am not a brooch'

'No you are not.You are a corsage. My own little corsage.'

Demeter put her hands on Ossip's paws and looked into his eyes.

'Please.'

Ossip let a little silence enter the caravanette.

'OK, but we must have equal billing. On that I insist,

And then' said Ossip 'you come back to Pest with me.'

Ossip grinned.

'To give the performance of your life before the Hungarian Academy of Science

I want them to know what they missed when they chucked you out.

They are all crazy for Celina Dion.'

'Equal billing?'

'It's a deal.'

And with that Ossip set about eating the contents of the handbag.

News travels fast.

Unusual movements observed on the Hungarian border.

The delicatessen at the Thurrock Tesco devastated.

Overnight articulated trailers labelled Hungarocamion or just sporting the letter H had taken all available parking spaces in the small industrial hamlet of Thurrock.

Small cooking fires and camping gaz stoves were soon burning merrily away in the shadow of huge oil storage tanks.

Mothers of Hungary cooked and Fathers ate goulash and drank beer. kids coke and 'amburger nonstop.

The manager of a furniture superstore, detecting a P.R. moment, diverted trailers of bean bags and camping chairs to the Venue.

The bottled water arrived on the Portaloo trucks, the Portaloos on the water trucks.

Fed and watered the vast Hungarian encampment waited patiently or joined the queue for the much admired bean bag.

Meanwhile.

A high power meeting was taking place in a smoke filled hut by the shore of the Thames.

The big boss, for it was he, had arrived turbo-charged in his Mercedes-badged Zil-41041 his braces still under threat of dissolution.

He said 'I want Ossip now!' and banged the table once. 'You can't hold him prisoner,' and banged the table twice. 'He is a Hungarian citizen!'

The table gave up and collapsed in a heap. The braces collapsed. Traditional Magyar leather trousers started to slide down.

'It was bound to happen' said Ossip 'In the country that gave birth to Isaac Newton.'

The lady mayoress hid behind her chain of office.

And tried to remember when she had last seen a half naked Hungarian.

'Maybe if you held the concerto far out on the marshes.' she ventured.

'No' declared the other chain-smoking lady present. In her broken Polish she said.

'From the heart lady mayor, from the heart I have fought for a home for my karaoke girls and now I have found it.

Its not my fault if my new Venue is situated directly under your bridge Mr Toll Master.

It is not my fault that Demeter and Ossip are a legend in Pest and for that matter Hungary.'

'But you can't move in the venue. There are Hungarians everywhere.'

The two ladies decided

Demeter would have to perform her Celina Dion impressions outside on the flat tin roof of the Venue, Ossip on windup gramophone.

The Toll Master said nothing. It later emerged he was in a syndicate betting on the length of the tailback from the bridge. The Chief Constable who was dressed quite fetchingly in a police woman's uniform (it later turned out she was a woman) twirled her moustache and said 'The country is closing down. the traffic tail has nearly touched the head.

London is surrounded.

We are having to helicopter in fried chicken and chips. The cooks at Scotland Yard are near collapse.'

The Toll Master gave a small pirouette of glee and started planning the extension to his villa in Marbella.

Serried lines of pot-bellied mustachioed Hungarian lorry drivers began a stomp.

De-meter..Ossip

De meter..Ossip

De meter..Ossip

It was time.

The small Polish lady was now chain-smoking on the roof of the Venue and supervising an improvised sound system capable of reaching the limits of Hungarian occupied Thurrock.

The speaker system gave an awful whine and burst into the sound of something being pushed up the other side of the bridge. All eyes turned to the crest . A black hand-painted Volkswagen caravanette came into view and started a long accelerating roll to the bottom of the bridge and the Venue. Who is it?

What is it?

Its RUBIC'S DUDES. Famous Hungarian backing group.

'Wowy.' cried Ossip and with a little push helped the windup gramophone into the river Thames.

'About time too.' said the Polish lady as they bundled the group, in their familiar dark glasses greased back hair and suits made up of colourful rubic squares of hand tailored cloth, onto the roof.

The lady mayoress followed them up the ladder. After making a speech in a Thurrock dialect of Hungarian which translated to 'see you in the dog and goose after the show', she presented the group with a large bowl of genuine American chewing gum to see them through the concerto.

The stomping lorry drivers were getting restless. The big boss stood in the centre of the roof, called for calm raising one arm while the other held his trousers in place.

A couple of temporarily redundant traffic police men turned their emergency super halogen lights on as

trembling as much with relief as anticipation Demeter stepped gingerly out of the shadows of the bridge on to the Venue roof in her silver and diamante roman sandals.

Blond black eyed red lipped with a small animated corsage nestling in the top of her tunic dress of pink sequins

She looked amazed at her massive audience and said in her best Hungarian 'You make me alive. Thank you.'

She reached centre stage and started to sing

YOU AND I WERE MEANT TO FLY.

Suddenly we were seeing Celina. Demeter had disappeared. Ossip gone.

He had spotted a battered old brass tube that might be his lost telescope.

Demeter in her Celina trance continue to wow her transfixed audience with hits …….ALONE …..WHEN I NEED YOU…….EYES ON ME…..I SURRENDER….ALL BY MYSELF…BECAUSE YOU LOVED ME.

'She will burn up that girl.' muttered the Polish lady.

'Its not my idea of a concerto.' said the lady mayoress. 'But' she added 'its very nice.' and glanced proprietorially at the big boss jury-rigging his trousers with best Thurrock string.

The big boss handed Demeter a drink.

'You OK?'

'Yeah but I can't stop.' she smiled back.

Turned once again to her adoring audience and sang ..I WANT YOU TO NEED ME and an ecstatic I AM YOUR ANGEL.......then THE POWER OF LOVE

Even Ossip was distracted from his observation of Polaris.

It was midnight. The concert was over.

The encores commenced…A NEW DAY HAS COME

….MY HEART WILL GO ON

But Demeter knew.

She watched the big boss.

Between numbers he said

'You will collapse.

One more and then you are gone ….OK?'

She nodded and sung I DROVE ALL NIGHT

And was gone.

When her audience realised….they gave the great Magyar howl last heard by Genghis Khan.

It was two hours past midnight.

Ossip took bow after bow.

The Hungarocamions started to roar for their cargoes

who lined up in in alternate sleeping and singing battalions for the journey to Pest and the Danube.

As the bridge returned to normal Ossip helped the RUBIC'S DUDES push their caravanette to its apex and watched as the first rays of sunlight illuminated their rapid descent through the hastily opened tolls and on in a cloud of burning engine oil.

He went in search of Demeter.

The big boss stopped him with a kind hand.

'Demeter is asleep in her caravan.

Come with me. We have work to do. Have you ever ridden in a Zil Ossip?'

It was afternoon when the big boss hitched the sleeping Demeter's caravan to his Zil.

He glanced proudly at his handiwork.

A newly-painted sign attached to the shed by the river announced it as THE ANGLO THURROCK PEST FRIENDSHIP SOCIETY

In the doorway wiping away a tear from her blushing cheeks stood the lady mayoress.

'Wait for me.' he called in Hungarian. 'I will be back as soon as I have changed my braces'……..another cloud of exhaust smoke and they were off into the long slow queue up the bridge and beyond .

Poor Demeter she woke up speeding along the autobahn covered in smuts.

'Don't let anybody tell you caravans don't bounce.' she was heard to mutter some 1000 km later as they processed through lines of lorry drivers into the big boss's transport yard on the banks of the Danube.

Smiling masseuses from the nearby thermal baths advanced on the caravan

'Come mamoushka.'

they crooned

'let wash you.'

'let clean you

and rub you with oils for'

they said with a flourish of bathing towels

'you are our princess.'

The Corps of Bathing Maidens, as they were known, seized the exhausted Demeter and carried her triumphantly off to their thermal baths.

LA PROMENADE.   LA PROMENADE.   LA PROMENADE.

But let us return to the yard.

Consternation in the office.

As the big boss entered he was amazed to see a full Cossack General and his staff drunkenly sprawled around the room.

'Comrade we have come for Celina.'

'Certainly comrade general but first I must find my spare braces.'

Which fortunately were in the same drawer that Ossip was sleeping in.

'Ask Demeter if she is prepared to go with a band of drunken Cossacks to the Ukraine,' the big boss muttered.

'I think the answer is no.' thought Ossip.

And scampered over a sodden Cossack in the direction of the caravanette.

Which,

oh dear,

was empty except for a jar of special Buda honey with the words FOR OSSIP written in Demeters inimitable scrawl on the label.

'I have some honey but no Demeter.'

'Celina. Its Celina as far as the general is concerned.' the big boss whispered urgently.

'Whass that?

Have a cigar.'

drawled the General.

'Celina says you are not drunk enough

To appreciate her singing.'

'She says give them more vodka.' said Ossip

Tossing bottles into the waiting cossack hands

'Drink'.

'She says after the juggling but before the dancing mon general.' confided the big boss.

(If they could ever find her in greater Buda and Pest)

and if she says no?

Then it will be a fraternal fight to the death

Hungarian lorry drivers (SOBER)versus Russian Cossacks (DRUNK)

DEAD DRUNK said Ossip throwing out another box of bottles.

'You find Demeter. I will do the juggling and Gravell can serve the drinks' said the big boss and Ossip in unison.

Well at least we are agreed about something

'Gravell' they bawled and commenced the great Hungarian Rubic Juggle one cube to every three bottles 2 juggler model.

Designed to make you cross eyed confided the inventor from deep in the 40ft trailer of rubic cubes where he was helping Ossip unravel the work of Care in the Community.

Guess who won the fight for fight there was when the vodka ran out and Celina did not run in.

Total radio silence, US surveillance noted, in Hungarian Sector.

The Nuclear Crisis Committee convened in the Kremlin.

An executive jet was scrambled .

The President of Hungary silently thanked his tailor, for making him pyjamas in the form of a three piece suit, as he greeted the Russian Chief of Staff.

'Aah a Zil' said the Chief of Staff and for the first time that morning smiled.

'Have a cigar Comrade President'.

'Let us drive to the transport yard'.

You could for want of a name call it a yard if you included the lorries floating amongst the debris in the Danube .

The Mayor of Budapest pulled at his beard and moustache. 'This is an ecological disaster' he repeated in various forms of wail while two rutting stags, the Cossack General(two black eyes) and the big boss (two black eyes), circled around the mayor ready for their next encounter.

All around them the minor contestants attempted the odd punch or kick mainly at the paramedics carrying them away.

'This calls for an immediate conference call.' said the chief of staff. 'get me Moscow'

The big boss who knew the score said 'We have no vodka.'

'Then it will have to be a serious conference. Turn off the commentary now.'

When we were turned back on again what changes had been made.

A labour battalion had flown in from Siberia and parachuted down to clear the Danube and rebuild the yard.

Vodka supplies had been renewed.

The mayor had eaten his beard …lost some bet or other….

And most importantly Demeter had been found, where else but on the stage at the Hungarian Academy of Sciences rehearsing for what she in her innocence thought was her next show.

No! non! no!

All the major players were crowded into the caravan in the corner of the yard by the Danube.

The chief of staff sat on the Cossack General's knee.

'But the Cossack tribes are gathering on the Ukraine border Celina.'

pleaded the now sober General.'What can I tell them?'

'You have suffered before. You will suffer again' said Demeter

At that the General said

'Oh this is insufferable'

and went to stand up As he did the Chief of Staff, known as Comrade Fatty in the Kremlin, fell off his knee and rolled across the floor hitting the wall, which was next to the Danube, a great thump.

In the confusion that followed the rest of the meeting rushed to the Chief of Staff's aid causing the centre of gravity (as Ossip explained in a later paper to the Hungarian Institute of Science) to alter to the general disadvantage as the caravan slowly rolled over into the river.

A moment of shock as the murky green water sucked the caravan down into its depths

And then

Out of the black sky blazing with searchlights roared a YAK24 helicopter from which leapt a stick of elite marine spetnatz frogmen.

'May all your yurts be big ones' cried the cheering lorry drivers.

'Now you sing for us I think' said General Fatty as he lay by Demeter. Lady masseuses rythmically pumping the Danube out of them.

So it came to pas

that the Cossack General,

sporting a monocle, his Bandoliers polished to a mirror finish and newly stocked by rare Hungarian Gallop cigars,

had the honor to command a military caravanette that carried the alcoholic remains of his general staff out through the plains of north Hungary to the gathering of the Cossack Natio

Cloaked in black, her blonde hair
bound in plaits a sheaf of summer
maize in her arms, Demeter
stepped from her caravanette and
strode in golden sandals, her
head held high, onto a great
round stage supported by a
mound of logs

She stood aside while the
Ukrainian Rubic Dude tribute
band fussed themselves into
some kind of order.

The big boss dropped his uplifted
arm.

A searchlight of sun burst into the sky. Lasers spattered strings of colour. The Cossacks roared.

Demeter motioned for silence. Shed her black cloak of winter.

The goddess of spring burst into song.

Ossip contemplating his pot of Buda honey

thought this better than Thurrock....well as good as.